Great Works

Instructional (...) for Literature

THE LION, THE WITCH AND THE WARDROBE

A guide for the novel by C.S. Lewis
Great Works Author: Kristin Kemp

SHELL EDUCATION

Image Credits

Shutterstock (cover; pages 1, 11)

Standards

© 2007 Teachers of English to Speakers of Other Languages, Inc. (TESOL)
© 2007 Board of Regents of the University of Wisconsin System. World-Class Instructional Design and Assessment (WIDA)
© Copyright 2010. National Governors Association Center for Best Practices and Council of Chief State School Officers. All rights reserved.

Shell Education

5301 Oceanus Drive
Huntington Beach, CA 92649-1030
http://www.shelleducation.com
ISBN 978-1-4807-6913-7
© 2015 Shell Educational Publishing, Inc.

Table of Contents

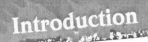

How to Use This Literature Guide

Today's standards demand rigor and relevance in the reading of complex texts. The units in this series guide teachers in a rich and deep exploration of worthwhile works of literature for classroom study. The most rigorous instruction can also be interesting and engaging!

Many current strategies for effective literacy instruction have been incorporated into these instructional guides for literature. Throughout the units, text-dependent questions are used to determine comprehension of the book as well as student interpretation of the vocabulary words. The books chosen for the series are complex exemplars of carefully crafted works of literature. Close reading is used throughout the units to guide students toward revisiting the text and using textual evidence to respond to prompts orally and in writing. Students must analyze the story elements in multiple assignments for each section of the book. All of these strategies work together to rigorously guide students through their study of literature.

The next few pages will make clear how to use this guide for a purposeful and meaningful literature study. Each section of this guide is set up in the same way to make it easier for you to implement the instruction in your classroom.

Theme Thoughts

The great works of literature used throughout this series have important themes that have been relevant to people for many years. Many of the themes will be discussed during the various sections of this instructional guide. However, it would also benefit students to have independent time to think about the key themes of the novel.

Before students begin reading, have them complete *Pre-Reading Theme Thoughts* (page 13). This graphic organizer will allow students to think about the themes outside the context of the story. They'll have the opportunity to evaluate statements based on important themes and defend their opinions. Be sure to have students keep their papers for comparison to the *Post-Reading Theme Thoughts* (page 64). This graphic organizer is similar to the pre-reading activity. However, this time, students will be answering the questions from the point of view of one of the characters in the novel. They have to think about how the character would feel about each statement and defend their thoughts. To conclude the activity, have students compare what they thought about the themes before they read the novel to what the characters discovered during the story.

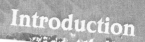

How to Use This Literature Guide *(cont.)*

Vocabulary

Each teacher overview page has definitions and sentences about how key vocabulary words are used in the section. These words should be introduced and discussed with students. There are two student vocabulary activity pages in each section. On the first page, students are asked to define the ten words chosen by the author of this unit. On the second page in most sections, each student will select at least eight words that he or she finds interesting or difficult. For each section, choose one of these pages for your students to complete. With either assignment, you may want to have students get into pairs to discuss the meanings of the words. Allow students to use reference guides to define the words. Monitor students to make sure the definitions they have found are accurate and relate to how the words are used in the text.

On some of the vocabulary student pages, students are asked to answer text-related questions about the vocabulary words. The following question stems will help you create your own vocabulary questions if you'd like to extend the discussion.

- How does this word describe _____'s character?
- In what ways does this word relate to the problem in this story?
- How does this word help you understand the setting?
- In what ways is this word related to the story's solution?
- Describe how this word supports the novel's theme of . . . .
- What visual images does this word bring to your mind?
- For what reasons might the author have chosen to use this particular word?

At times, more work with the words will help students understand their meanings. The following quick vocabulary activities are a good way to further study the words.

- Have students practice their vocabulary and writing skills by creating sentences and/or paragraphs in which multiple vocabulary words are used correctly and with evidence of understanding.
- Students can play vocabulary concentration. Students make a set of cards with the words and a separate set of cards with the definitions. Then, students lay the cards out on the table and play concentration. The goal of the game is to match vocabulary words with their definitions.
- Students can create word journal entries about the words. Students choose words they think are important and then describe why they think each word is important within the novel.

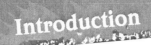

How to Use This Literature Guide (cont.)

Analyzing the Literature

After students have read each section, hold small-group or whole-class discussions. Questions are written at two levels of complexity to allow you to decide which questions best meet the needs of your students. The Level 1 questions are typically less abstract than the Level 2 questions. Level 1 is indicated by a square, while Level 2 is indicated by a triangle. These questions focus on the various story elements, such as character, setting, and plot. Student pages are provided if you want to assign these questions for individual student work before your group discussion. Be sure to add further questions as your students discuss what they've read. For each question, a few key points are provided for your reference as you discuss the novel with students.

Reader Response

In today's classrooms, there are often great readers who are below-average writers. So much time and energy is spent in classrooms getting students to read on grade level that little time is left to focus on writing skills. To help teachers include more writing in their daily literacy instruction, each section of this guide has a literature-based reader response prompt. Each of the three genres of writing is used in the reader responses within this guide: narrative, informative/explanatory, and argument. Students have a choice between two prompts for each reader response. One response requires students to make connections between the reading and their own lives. The other prompt requires students to determine text-to-text connections or connections within the text.

Close Reading the Literature

Within each section, students are asked to closely reread a short section of text. Since some versions of the novels have different page numbers, the selections are described by chapter and location, along with quotations to guide the readers. After each close reading, there are text-dependent questions to be answered by students.

Encourage students to read each question one at a time and then go back to the text and discover the answer. Work with students to ensure that they use the text to determine their answers rather than making unsupported inferences. Once students have answered the questions, discuss what they discovered. Suggested answers are provided in the answer key.

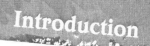

How to Use This Literature Guide (cont.)

Close Reading the Literature (cont.)

The generic, open-ended stems below can be used to write your own text-dependent questions if you would like to give students more practice.

- Give evidence from the text to support . . . .
- Justify your thinking using text evidence about . . . .
- Find evidence to support your conclusions about . . . .
- What text evidence helps the reader understand . . . ?
- Use the book to tell why _____ happens.
- Based on events in the story, ...
- Use text evidence to describe why . . . .

Making Connections

The activities in this section help students make cross-curricular connections to writing, mathematics, science, social studies, or the fine arts. Each of these types of activities requires higher-order thinking skills from students.

Creating with the Story Elements

It is important to spend time discussing the common story elements in literature. Understanding the characters, setting, and plot can increase students' comprehension and appreciation of the story. If teachers discuss these elements daily, students will more likely internalize the concepts and look for the elements in their independent reading. Another important reason for focusing on the story elements is that students will be better writers if they think about how the stories they read are constructed.

Students are given three options for working with the story elements. They are asked to create something related to the characters, setting, or plot of the novel. Students are given a choice in this activity so that they can decide to complete the activity that most appeals to them. Different multiple intelligences are used so that the activities are diverse and interesting to all students.

How to Use This Literature Guide (cont.)

Culminating Activity

This open-ended, cross-curricular activity requires higher-order thinking and allows for a creative product. Students will enjoy getting the chance to share what they have discovered through reading the novel. Be sure to allow them enough time to complete the activity at school or home.

Comprehension Assessment

The questions in this section are modeled after current standardized tests to help students analyze what they've read and prepare for tests they may see in their classrooms. The questions are dependent on the text and require critical-thinking skills to answer.

Response to Literature

The final post-reading activity is an essay based on the text that also requires further research by students. This is a great way to extend this book into other curricular areas. A suggested rubric is provided for teacher reference.

Correlation to the Standards

Shell Education is committed to producing educational materials that are research and standards based. As part of this effort, we have correlated all of our products to the academic standards of all 50 states, the District of Columbia, the Department of Defense Dependents Schools, and all Canadian provinces.

Purpose and Intent of Standards

Standards are designed to focus instruction and guide adoption of curricula. Standards are statements that describe the criteria necessary for students to meet specific academic goals. They define the knowledge, skills, and content students should acquire at each level. Standards are also used to develop standardized tests to evaluate students' academic progress. Teachers are required to demonstrate how their lessons meet standards. Standards are used in the development of all of our products, so educators can be assured they meet high academic standards.

How to Find Standards Correlations

To print a customized correlation report of this product for your state, visit our website at http://www.shelleducation.com and follow the online directions. If you require assistance in printing correlation reports, please contact our Customer Service Department at 1-877-777-3450.

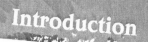

Correlation to the Standards (cont.)

Standards Correlation Chart

The lessons in this guide were written to support the Common Core College and Career Readiness Anchor Standards. This chart indicates which sections of this guide address the anchor standards.

Common Core College and Career Readiness Anchor Standard	Section
CCSS.ELA-Literacy.CCRA.R.1—Read closely to determine what the text says explicitly and to make logical inferences from it; cite specific textual evidence when writing or speaking to support conclusions drawn from the text.	Analyzing the Literature Sections 1–5; Close Reading the Literature Sections 1–5; Making Connections Section 1; Creating with the Story Elements Sections 1–5; Post-Reading Response to Literature
CCSS.ELA-Literacy.CCRA.R.2—Determine central ideas or themes of a text and analyze their development; summarize the key supporting details and ideas.	Analyzing the Literature Sections 1–5; Reader Response Sections 1–5; Post-Reading Response to Literature
CCSS.ELA-Literacy.CCRA.R.3—Analyze how and why individuals, events, or ideas develop and interact over the course of a text.	Analyzing the Literature Sections 1–5; Creating with the Story Elements Section 5
CCSS.ELA-Literacy.CCRA.R.4—Interpret words and phrases as they are used in a text, including determining technical, connotative, and figurative meanings, and analyze how specific word choices shape meaning or tone.	Vocabulary Sections 1–5
CCSS.ELA-Literacy.CCRA.R.10—Read and comprehend complex literary and informational texts independently and proficiently.	Analyzing the Literature Sections 1–5; Reader Response Sections 1–5; Close Reading the Literature Sections 1–5; Post-Reading Response to Literature
CCSS.ELA-Literacy.CCRA.W.1—Write arguments to support claims in an analysis of substantive topics or texts using valid reasoning and relevant and sufficient evidence.	Reader Response Sections 1, 2, 4, 5; Post-Reading Response to Literature
CCSS.ELA-Literacy.CCRA.W.2—Write informative/explanatory texts to examine and convey complex ideas and information clearly and accurately through the effective selection, organization, and analysis of content.	Reader Response Sections 1, 3, 5; Making Connections Section 5; Post-Reading Response to Literature
CCSS.ELA-Literacy.CCRA.W.3—Write narratives to develop real or imagined experiences or events using effective technique, well-chosen details and well-structured event sequences.	Reader Response Sections 2, 3, 4
CCSS.ELA-Literacy.CCRA.W.4—Produce clear and coherent writing in which the development, organization, and style are appropriate to task, purpose, and audience.	Reader Response Sections 1–5; Making Connections Section 3; Culminating Activity; Post-Reading Response to Literature
CCSS.ELA-Literacy.CCRA.W.5—Develop and strengthen writing as needed by planning, revising, editing, rewriting, or trying a new approach.	Culminating Activity

Correlation to the Standards (cont.)

Standards Correlation Chart (cont.)

Common Core College and Career Readiness Anchor Standard	Section
CCSS.ELA-Literacy.CCRA.W.7—Conduct short as well as more sustained research projects based on focused questions, demonstrating understanding of the subject under investigation.	Making Connections Section 4; Post-Reading Response to Literature
CCSS.ELA-Literacy.CCRA.L.1—Demonstrate command of the conventions of standard English grammar and usage when writing or speaking.	Reader Response Sections 1–5; Close Reading the Literature Sections 1–5; Culminating Activity; Post-Reading Response to Literature
CCSS.ELA-Literacy.CCRA.L.2—Demonstrate command of the conventions of standard English capitalization, punctuation, and spelling when writing.	Reader Response Sections 1–5; Close Reading the Literature Sections 1–5; Culminating Activity; Post-Reading Response to Literature
CCSS.ELA-Literacy.CCRA.L.3—Apply knowledge of language to understand how language functions in different contexts, to make effective choices for meaning or style, and to comprehend more fully when reading or listening.	Reader Response Sections 1–5; Making Connections Section 3; Post-Reading Response to Literature
CCSS.ELA-Literacy.CCRA.L.4—Determine or clarify the meaning of unknown and multiple-meaning words and phrases by using context clues, analyzing meaningful word parts, and consulting general and specialized reference materials, as appropriate.	Vocabulary Sections 1–5
CCSS.ELA-Literacy.CCRA.L.5—Demonstrate understanding of figurative language, word relationships, and nuances in word meanings.	Making Connections Section 3
CCSS.ELA-Literacy.CCRA.L.6—Acquire and use accurately a range of general academic and domain-specific words and phrases sufficient for reading, writing, speaking, and listening at the college and career readiness level; demonstrate independence in gathering vocabulary knowledge when encountering an unknown term important to comprehension or expression.	Vocabulary Sections 1–5

TESOL and WIDA Standards

The lessons in this book promote English language development for English language learners. The following TESOL and WIDA English Language Development Standards are addressed through the activities in this book:

- Standard 1: English language learners communicate for social and instructional purposes within the school setting.
- Standard 2: English language learners communicate information, ideas and concepts necessary for academic success in the content area of language arts.

About the Author—C.S. Lewis

Clive Staples Lewis, known as C.S. Lewis to most of the world and Jack to his friends, was born on November 29, 1898, in Ireland. His mother passed away when he was nine, and his father sent him to three different boarding schools with his older brother, Warren. Brought up in a strict, religious home, Lewis denounced Christianity as a young teenager.

He served in the British Army during World War I and was an English Language and Literature tutor at Oxford University for 29 years. Through his friendships with a few men, including J.R.R. Tolkien (author of The Lord of the Rings trilogy), Lewis embraced Christianity as an adult and went on to write over 30 books, dozens of essays and articles, and many radio addresses, most of which are about theology.

Lewis published the children's book *The Lion, the Witch and the Wardrobe* in 1950. Over the next few years, he wrote the other six books in the Chronicles of Narnia series. These books have sold over 100 million copies, been translated into over 47 languages, and been adapted into major motion pictures.

In 1956, Lewis married Joy Davidman, an American diagnosed with terminal cancer and facing deportation. Her health improved, and they enjoyed a few years of marriage before her cancer returned. She passed away in 1960. Lewis was diagnosed with kidney problems in 1961, and he died on November 22, 1963. This was the same day President John F. Kennedy was assassinated.

Lewis is considered by many to be one of the greatest thinkers and writers of the twentieth century, and his beloved Chronicles of Narnia series has solidified his seat among the greats of children's literature.

Possible Texts for Text Comparisons

The other books in the Chronicles of Narnia series could be used as enriching text comparisons. The additional titles are *Prince Caspian*, *The Voyage of the Dawn Treader*, *The Silver Chair*, *The Horse and His Boy*, *The Magician's Nephew*, and *The Last Battle*.

Book Summary of *The Lion, the Witch and the Wardrobe*

During the British air raids of World War II, siblings Peter, Susan, Edmund, and Lucy Pevensie are sent to the English countryside to stay in a huge old mansion with an eccentric professor. While playing hide-and-seek, the youngest, Lucy, discovers another world—Narnia—through the back of a wardrobe. Narnia is a fantasy land under the spell of the evil White Witch, who has made it always winter but never Christmas. The others initially do not believe her, but eventually her brother, Edmund, finds his way through the wardrobe and into the carriage of the Witch herself.

Edmund, a sullen child, makes a deal with the Witch to bring his brother and sisters to her in exchange for being made a prince. When all four siblings finally make their way into Narnia, they learn of Aslan, the true King who has been away for a long time, and of a legend foretelling the downfall of the Witch's power when four human children enter Narnia.

As Aslan approaches, changes come with him. Christmas finally comes with an appearance by Father Christmas handing out gifts, and the frozen winter begins to melt into spring. Aslan arrives, and Edmund's betrayal is discovered. The Witch says Edmund must die, but Aslan sacrifices himself so Edmund will be spared. After Aslan's death, he comes back to life and the Witch's power is defeated in a great battle. The children stay in Narnia as Kings and Queens through adulthood until they finally find their way back through the wardrobe and into the regular world. They are children once more, and it is the very same afternoon on which they left.

In citing his inspiration for *The Lion, the Witch and the Wardrobe*, Lewis stated that for years he had a picture in his mind of a faun walking in the snow and carrying a package and an umbrella. That simple image sparked not only the beloved children's classic, but eventually the entire Chronicles of Narnia series.

Cross-Curricular Connection

This book could be used in a science unit on the tundra or climate change, a social studies unit on World War II in Europe, or a language arts or art unit on mythical creatures.

Possible Texts for Text Sets

- Cole, Joanna. *The Magic School Bus and the Climate Challenge*. Scholastic, 2010.
- Larios, Julie. *Imaginary Menagerie: A Book of Curious Creatures*. Harcourt Children's Books, 2008.
- Lynch, Wayne. *The Arctic (Our Wild World)*. Cooper Square Publishing, LLC, 2007.
- Parsons, Martin. *Air Raids (The History Detective Investigates Britain at War)*. Wayland Publishing Ltd., 1999.

Name _____

Date _____

Pre-Reading Theme Thoughts

Directions: Read each of the statements in the first column. Decide if you agree or disagree with the statements. Record your opinion by marking an X in Agree or Disagree for each statement. Explain your choices in the fourth column. There are no right or wrong answers.

Statement	Agree	Disagree	Explain Your Answer
You should not believe something unless you see it for yourself.			
People who have done bad things should be forgiven.			
Sacrifice is a way to show love.			
Children are too young to do brave and noble things.			

Vocabulary Overview

Ten key words from this section are provided below with definitions and sentences about how the words are used in the book. Choose one of the vocabulary activity sheets (pages 15 or 16) for students to complete as they read this section. Monitor students as they work to ensure that the definitions they have found are accurate and relate to the text. Finally, discuss these important vocabulary words with students. If you think these words or other words in the section warrant more time devoted to them, there are suggestions in the introduction for other vocabulary activities (page 5).

Word	Definition	Sentence about Text
row (ch. 1)	a noisy disturbance or quarrel	Lucy says there will be a **row** if the children are heard talking.
wireless (ch. 1)	an old-fashioned British word for radio	The children will not be bored because the house has a **wireless** and lots of books.
inquisitive (ch. 1)	very curious	Lucy feels frightened but also **inquisitive** about going through the wardrobe.
melancholy (ch. 2)	a sad mood or feeling	Mr. Tumnus speaks with a **melancholy** voice.
cloven (ch. 2)	an animal's hoof divided into two parts	Mr. Tumnus is worried the Witch will turn his **cloven** hoofs into solid ones.
hoax (ch. 3)	an act meant to trick someone	When Lucy shares about Narnia, Peter says it is a good **hoax**.
spiteful (ch. 3)	wanting to hurt or anger someone	Edmund is **spiteful** toward Lucy and teases her about Narnia.
sledge (ch. 3)	a vehicle on runners used for carrying loads or people over ice and snow; a sleigh	Edmund sees a **sledge** pulled by white reindeer.
dominions (ch. 4)	territories a ruler or government controls	The Witch asks Edmund how he came to enter her **dominions**.
flushed (ch. 4)	a reddening of the face because of sickness or emotion	Lucy does not notice Edmund has a **flushed** face.

Name _____

Date _____

Understanding Vocabulary Words

Directions: The following words appear in this section of the book. Use context clues and reference materials to determine an accurate definition for each word.

Word	Definition
row (ch. 1)	
wireless (ch. 1)	
inquisitive (ch. 1)	
melancholy (ch. 2)	
cloven (ch. 2)	
hoax (ch. 3)	
spiteful (ch. 3)	
sledge (ch. 3)	
dominions (ch. 4)	
flushed (ch. 4)	

Name _____

Date _____

During-Reading Vocabulary Activity

Directions: As you read these chapters, record at least eight important words on the lines below. Try to find interesting, difficult, intriguing, special, or funny words. Your words can be long or short. They can be hard or easy to spell. After each word, use context clues in the text and reference materials to define the word.

- _____
- _____
- _____
- _____
- _____
- _____
- _____
- _____
- _____
- _____
- _____

Directions: Respond to these questions about the words in this section.

1. Why does Mr. Tumnus speak with a **melancholy** voice?

_____

_____

2. What makes Peter think Lucy's story is a **hoax**?

_____

_____

Analyzing the Literature

Provided below are discussion questions you can use in small groups, with the whole class, or for written assignments. Each question is given at two levels so you can choose the right question for each group of students. Activity sheets with these questions are provided (pages 18–19) if you want students to write their responses. For each question, a few key discussion points are provided for your reference.

Story Element	■ Level 1	▲ Level 2	Key Discussion Points
Plot	What is the real reason Mr. Tumnus takes Lucy to his home during her first visit?	Why does Mr. Tumnus become so upset during his first visit with Lucy?	Mr. Tumnus is a hired kidnapper for the Witch. If he ever sees a human boy or girl, he is to bring him/her to the Witch at once. He is upset because he likes Lucy and knows it would be wrong to hand her over to the Witch.
Plot	Explain what happens when Lucy tries to show her siblings the way to Narnia.	Under what circumstances do you think the wardrobe will lead to Narnia?	The wardrobe led nowhere when she tries to show her siblings. Peter raps his knuckles against the back of it, and it is solid wood. Students may have a variety of guesses, but a couple of examples are: it only leads to Narnia for one person at a time or only when it is raining.
Character	How does Edmund respond to Lucy's story of visiting Narnia?	Compare and contrast Edmund's response to Lucy's story of visiting Narnia to that of Peter's and Susan's.	Edmund doesn't believe Lucy and teases her about it, often being rude and spiteful. Peter and Susan also do not believe her, but they do not go on about it and do not make her feel so badly about it.
Setting	Describe the weather of Narnia.	Describe the weather of Narnia and explain the reason for it being that way.	Narnia is described as being very cold and snowy. It is "always winter, but never Christmas." The Witch has Narnia under a spell that causes such weather.

Name _____

Date _____

■ Analyzing the Literature

Directions: Think about the section you just read. Read each question and state your response with textual evidence.

1. What is the real reason Mr. Tumnus takes Lucy to his home during her first visit?

   _____

   _____

   _____

   _____

2. Explain what happens when Lucy tries to show her siblings the way to Narnia.

   _____

   _____

   _____

   _____

3. How does Edmund respond to Lucy's story of visiting Narnia?

   _____

   _____

   _____

   _____

4. Describe the weather of Narnia.

   _____

   _____

   _____

   _____

Name _____

Date _____

▲ Analyzing the Literature

Directions: Think about the section you just read. Read each question and state your response with textual evidence.

1. Why does Mr. Tumnus become so upset during his first visit with Lucy?

_____

_____

_____

_____

2. Under what circumstances do you think the wardrobe will lead to Narnia?

_____

_____

_____

_____

3. Compare and contrast Edmund's response to Lucy's story of visiting Narnia to that of Peter's and Susan's.

_____

_____

_____

_____

4. Describe the weather of Narnia and explain the reason for it being that way.

_____

_____

_____

_____

Name _____

Date _____

Reader Response

Directions: Choose one of the following prompts about this section to answer. Be sure you include a topic sentence in your response, use textual evidence to support your opinion, and provide a strong conclusion that summarizes your opinion.

Writing Prompts

- **Informative/Explanatory Piece**—If you were Lucy, explain how you would convince your siblings you were telling the truth about Narnia.
- **Opinion/Argument Piece**—Now that Edmund has also visited Narnia, how do you think Peter and Susan might respond? Use information about their characters in your response.

_____

_____

_____

_____

_____

_____

_____

_____

_____

_____

_____

_____

_____

_____

Name _____

Date _____

Close Reading the Literature

Directions: Closely reread the section in chapter 4 when Edmund meets the Witch. Begin with, "At last the Turkish Delight was all finished . . . ." Stop when the Witch leaves, saying, "Don't forget. Come soon." Read each question and then revisit the text to find evidence that supports your answer.

1. Use the text to explain why Edmund wants more Turkish Delight.

   _____

   _____

   _____

   _____

2. Give an example from this section that shows that Edmund is selfish.

   _____

   _____

   _____

   _____

3. According to the text, how will Edmund find the Witch's castle?

   _____

   _____

   _____

4. What excuse does the Witch give Edmund to explain why Lucy might be afraid to see her?

   _____

   _____

   _____

Name _____

Date _____

Making Connections—British Air Raids

Directions: The Pevensie children go to the Professor's house because of the air raids in England during World War II. Read the information below. Then, answer the questions in complete sentences.

During World War II, enemy planes dropped bombs on big cities in England, like London. When people heard a loud siren, they knew danger was coming, so they would go to shelters. Many people had shelters in their homes. An outdoor shelter was called an *Anderson shelter*. It was built under a garden and had wavy steel walls for strength. Indoor shelters were called *Morrison shelters*. These were steel tables with cage-like sides. Public shelters were made of brick but were not as strong.

Many parents were worried about their children. During the war, over 800,000 children were evacuated, or removed from danger. Most went to the country. Sometimes, the children lived with family or friends. More often, though, they lived with volunteer families they did not know. Some of the children stayed only a few weeks, but others remained until the war was over.

1. Compare and contrast the Anderson and Morrison shelters.

   _____

   _____

   _____

2. Why were children evacuated from big cities?

   _____

   _____

3. What problems do you think the evacuated children faced?

   _____

   _____

   _____

Name _____

Date _____

Creating with the Story Elements

Directions: Thinking about the story elements of character, setting, and plot in a novel is very important to understanding what is happening and why. Complete **one** of the following activities based on what you've read so far. Be creative and have fun!

Characters

Choose Lucy, Edmund, Mr. Tumnus, or the Witch to use in a character web. Put the character in the middle and web two different traits about him or her. For each trait, give one example from the book that supports it. For example, if you were webbing about Susan, you could say she is optimistic because she thinks the rain will stop quickly.

Setting

Draw a picture of Mr. Tumnus's home in the cave. Use the descriptive details in the book and your imagination to add details to your drawing.

Plot

The Witch has Mr. Tumnus looking for "Daughters of Eve" and "Sons of Adam." Create a wanted poster she can hang on the trees in Narnia. At the bottom, write a prediction about why she wants to find them. Be creative and colorful!

Vocabulary Overview

Ten key words from this section are provided below with definitions and sentences about how the words are used in the book. Choose one of the vocabulary activity sheets (pages 25 or 26) for students to complete as they read this section. Monitor students as they work to ensure the definitions they have found are accurate and relate to the text. Finally, discuss these important vocabulary words with students. If you think these words or other words in the section warrant more time devoted to them, there are suggestions in the introduction for other vocabulary activities (page 5).

Word	Definition	Sentence about Text
reliable (ch. 5)	able to be trusted	The Professor asks whether Edmund or Lucy is more **reliable**.
logic (ch. 5)	a proper way to think about or understand something	The Professor wonders if the children are taught **logic** in school.
probable (ch. 5)	likely, but not certain, to be true	It is **probable** that there are other worlds around the corner.
resumed (ch. 6)	to begin again after stopping	After there is no more to say, the children **resume** their journey.
occupant (ch. 6)	a person living in a particular place	The former **occupant** of the cave is under arrest.
fraternizing (ch. 6)	to be friendly with someone	Mr. Tumnus is accused of **fraternizing** with humans.
alighted (ch. 6)	to land on a surface after flying	Snow falls off the branch as the robin **alights**.
boughs (ch. 7)	the main branches of a tree	The children talk to Mr. Beaver where the **boughs** of trees grow close together.
token (ch. 7)	an object serving as a visual symbol of a feeling or event	Mr. Beaver's **token** is Lucy's handkerchief.
modest (ch. 7)	not showing pride or arrogance	Mr. Beaver has a **modest** expression as he shows the children his dam.

Name _____

Date _____

Understanding Vocabulary Words

Directions: The following words appear in this section of the book. Use context clues and reference materials to determine an accurate definition for each word.

Word	Definition
reliable (ch. 5)	
logic (ch. 5)	
probable (ch. 5)	
resumed (ch. 6)	
occupant (ch. 6)	
fraternizing (ch. 6)	
alighted (ch. 6)	
boughs (ch. 7)	
token (ch. 7)	
modest (ch. 7)	

Name _____

Date _____

During-Reading Vocabulary Activity

Directions: As you read these chapters, record at least eight important words on the lines below. Try to find interesting, difficult, intriguing, special, or funny words. Your words can be long or short. They can be hard or easy to spell. After each word, use context clues in the text and reference materials to define the word.

- _____
- _____
- _____
- _____
- _____
- _____
- _____
- _____
- _____
- _____

Directions: Respond to these questions about the words in this section.

1. Why does the Professor wonder if **logic** is taught in schools?

   _____

   _____

2. Why do the children talk to Mr. Beaver under the **boughs** of the trees?

   _____

   _____

Analyzing the Literature

Provided below are discussion questions you can use in small groups, with the whole class, or for written assignments. Each question is given at two levels so you can choose the right question for each group of students. Activity sheets with these questions are provided (pages 28–29) if you want students to write their responses. For each question, a few key discussion points are provided for your reference.

Story Element	■ Level 1	▲ Level 2	Key Discussion Points
Character	What does Edmund tell Peter and Susan after he visits Narnia?	Why does Edmund lie about visiting Narnia?	Edmund lies and says he did not visit Narnia, and that he and Lucy were just playing. He lies because he is feeling annoyed that Lucy was right, and he wants to let her down.
Setting	What do the children find at Mr. Tumnus's home?	Why has Mr. Tumnus's home been wrecked?	Mr. Tumnus's cave is a mess. The door is hanging off its hinges, snow has drifted in, crockery is smashed and is lying on the floor, and his father's portrait has been slashed. This has happened because the Witch found out about his visit with Lucy and her guards have taken him.
Character	What is each child's reaction to hearing Aslan's name?	What does each child's reaction to Aslan's name tell about his or her character?	Edmund feels horror; Peter feels brave and adventurous; Susan feels as if a delicious smell or beautiful music floated by her; Lucy feels excitement like at the beginning of summer. Examples of what this could show about their characters are: Edmund is guilty of something; Peter is courageous; Susan is gentle; Lucy is cheerful.
Plot	What does Edmund notice in the distance when looking at Mr. Beaver's dam?	What horrible ideas do you think came into Edmund's head as he looked at the two hills in the distance?	Edmund notices the two hills the Witch told him about and realizes that her castle is there. Students' answers may vary, but an example is: The horrible ideas include bringing his brother and sisters to the Witch so he can be Prince and eat more Turkish Delight.

Name _____

Date _____

Analyzing the Literature

Directions: Think about the section you just read. Read each question and state your response with textual evidence.

1. What does Edmund tell Peter and Susan after he visits Narnia?

_____

_____

_____

_____

2. What do the children find at Mr. Tumnus's home?

_____

_____

_____

_____

3. What is each child's reaction to hearing Aslan's name?

_____

_____

_____

_____

4. What does Edmund notice in the distance when looking at Mr. Beaver's dam?

_____

_____

_____

_____

Name _____

Date _____

▲ Analyzing the Literature

Directions: Think about the section you just read. Read each question and state your response with textual evidence.

1. Why does Edmund lie about visiting Narnia?

_____

_____

_____

_____

2. Why has Mr. Tumnus's home been wrecked?

_____

_____

_____

_____

3. What does each child's reaction to Aslan's name tell about his or her character?

_____

_____

_____

_____

4. What horrible ideas do you think came into Edmund's head as he looked at the two hills in the distance?

_____

_____

_____

_____

Name _____

Date _____

Reader Response

Directions: Choose one of the following prompts about this section to answer. Be sure you include a topic sentence in your response, use textual evidence to support your opinion, and provide a strong conclusion that summarizes your opinion.

Writing Prompts

- **Opinion/Argument Piece**—When talking with the Professor, Peter says, "If things are real, they're there all the time." Do you agree or disagree with this statement? Use examples from the text or your own experiences to support your opinion.
- **Narrative Piece**—Pretend you are Edmund. Write a letter to the Witch explaining the "horrible ideas" that are in your head.

_____

_____

_____

_____

_____

_____

_____

_____

_____

_____

_____

_____

_____

Name _____

Date _____

Close Reading the Literature

Directions: Closely reread Peter and Susan's discussion with the Professor in chapter 5. Begin when the Professor says, "How do you know that your sister's story is not true?" Stop with, "And that was the end of the conversation." Read each question, and then revisit the text to find evidence that supports your answer.

1. According to the text, what is "a very serious thing; a very serious thing indeed."

   _____

   _____

   _____

2. What three logical possibilities does the Professor offer Peter and Susan about Lucy's story?

   _____

   _____

   _____

3. In the chapter, what detail of Lucy's story makes the Professor think it is likely to be true?

   _____

   _____

   _____

4. In the section, what is the Professor's plan that no one has suggested yet?

   _____

   _____

   _____

Name _____

Date _____

Making Connections–Build a Dam

Directions: Mr. Beaver is very proud of the dam he made. For a dam to be effective, it should be made of something that is not permeable. Permeable means "allowing liquids to pass through." Complete the experiment and fill out the table to find out which material makes the best dam. Then, answer the questions.

Materials

- plastic or foil container, about 8" x 8"
- water
- measuring cup
- gravel
- clay
- sand
- timer

Instructions

- Build a wall across the middle of the container using the gravel.
- Pour two cups of water into one side of the container.
- Use the timer to see how long it takes the water to seep through to the other side. Record it on the table.
- Empty the container and repeat for clay and sand.

Material	Time

1. Which material was most permeable? Least permeable?

   _____

   _____

2. What qualities affect how a material is permeable?

   _____

   _____

3. On another sheet of paper, answer the following question: What do you think would happen if you used all three materials to create a dam?

Name _____

Date _____

Creating with the Story Elements

Directions: Thinking about the story elements of character, setting, and plot in a novel is very important to understanding what is happening and why. Complete **one** of the following activities based on what you've read so far. Be creative and have fun!

Characters

Think about the Professor. Write down three quotations from him during his talk with Peter and Susan that give examples of his character.

Setting

Draw a map of Narnia including the places the children have seen or traveled to so far. Don't forget the wardrobe entrance and the lamp-post.

Plot

Mr. Tumnus gives Mr. Beaver Lucy's handkerchief as a token so the children will trust Mr. Beaver. Use information in the story and your imagination to write the dialogue that might have been spoken between these two characters when the token was passed along.

Vocabulary Overview

Ten key words from this section are provided below with definitions and sentences about how the words are used in the book. Choose one of the vocabulary activity sheets (pages 35 or 36) for students to complete as they read this section. Monitor students as they work to ensure the definitions they have found are accurate and relate to the text. Finally, discuss these important vocabulary words with students. If you think these words or other words in the section warrant more time devoted to them, there are suggestions in the introduction for other vocabulary activities (page 5).

Word	Definition	Sentence about Text
prophecy (ch. 8)	a prediction that something will happen in the future	The **prophecy** says there are four thrones for two Sons of Adam and two Daughters of Eve.
betrayed (ch. 8)	gave information to an enemy	Edmund goes to the Witch and has **betrayed** them all.
decoy (ch. 8)	something to attract people's attention so they will not notice something else	The Witch uses Edmund as a **decoy** or as bait to catch the others.
turret (ch. 9)	a small tower on a castle	Edmund walks past **turret** after turret to find the door to the Witch's castle.
mere (ch. 9)	small or unimportant	Edmund is frightened of a **mere** statue!
abide (ch. 10)	to be able to tolerate something	Mrs. Beaver cannot **abide** the idea of the Witch fiddling with her sewing machine.
plaguey (ch. 10)	annoying or troublesome	Everyone is in a **plaguey** mood, so Mrs. Beaver doesn't bring pillows.
sheath (ch. 10)	a protective covering for a sword	Father Christmas gives Peter a sword with a **sheath** and a belt.
gaiety (ch. 11)	happy and lively	The **gaiety** leaves the party members' faces when they see who is in the sledge.
gluttony (ch. 11)	eating or drinking too much	The Witch wants to know the meaning of the **gluttony** and waste.

Name _____

Date _____

Understanding Vocabulary Words

Directions: The following words appear in this section of the book. Use context clues and reference materials to determine an accurate definition for each word.

Word	Definition
prophecy (ch. 8)	
betrayed (ch. 8)	
decoy (ch. 8)	
turret (ch. 9)	
mere (ch. 9)	
abide (ch. 10)	
plaguey (ch. 10)	
sheath (ch. 10)	
gaiety (ch. 11)	
gluttony (ch. 11)	

Name _____

Date _____

During-Reading Vocabulary Activity

Directions: As you read these chapters, record at least eight important words on the lines below. Try to find interesting, difficult, intriguing, special, or funny words. Your words can be long or short. They can be hard or easy to spell. After each word, use context clues in the text and reference materials to define the word.

- _____

- _____

- _____

- _____

- _____

- _____

- _____

- _____

- _____

- _____

Directions: Now, organize your words. Rewrite each of your words on a sticky note. Work as a group to create a bar graph of your words. You should stack any words that are the same on top of one another. Different words appear in different columns. Finally, discuss with a group why certain words were chosen more often than other words.

Analyzing the Literature

Provided below are discussion questions you can use in small groups, with the whole class, or for written assignments. Each question is given at two levels so you can choose the right question for each group of students. Activity sheets with these questions are provided (pages 38–39) if you want students to write their responses. For each question, a few key discussion points are provided for your reference.

Story Element	■ Level 1	▲ Level 2	Key Discussion Points
Plot	What information do Mr. and Mrs. Beaver share about Aslan?	What do the children learn about Aslan and the Witch?	Aslan, a lion, is the true King of Narnia, but he hasn't been in Narnia for many years. A prophecy says that when he returns, he will right the wrongs in Narnia. The Witch says she is human, but she is actually part Jinn and part giant.
Character	What lies does Edmund tell himself as he walks to the Witch's castle?	Why does Edmund lie to himself on his way to the Witch's castle?	Edmund tells himself that the Witch wouldn't harm his siblings. The people saying mean things about her are her enemies, so it probably isn't true. He lies to himself because he knows the truth, but he wants to be a prince and eat Turkish Delight more than he wants to admit he is wrong.
Setting	Give examples from the story to show that the weather is changing.	Why is the changing of the weather so important in the story?	Examples in the story are: Father Christmas visits; the snow stops and melts; the temperature rises; and green trees, bushes, and flowers are seen. The importance of this is that it shows the Witch's spell is breaking now that Aslan is coming back, and the prophecy is beginning to come true.
Plot	Compare the way the Witch treats Edmund during their first and second meetings.	Why does the Witch treat Edmund so differently from their first meeting?	At first, the Witch is very kind to Edmund, but she is cruel during their second meeting. She gives him only water and stale bread and abuses him. In their first meeting she is only nice in order to get him to trust her. Now that he has returned to Narnia with his siblings, she can act however she wants.

Name _____

Date _____

Analyzing the Literature

Directions: Think about the section you just read. Read each question and state your response with textual evidence.

1. What information do Mr. and Mrs. Beaver share about Aslan?

_____

_____

_____

_____

2. What lies does Edmund tell himself as he walks to the Witch's castle?

_____

_____

_____

_____

3. Give examples from the story to show that the weather is changing.

_____

_____

_____

_____

4. Compare the way the Witch treats Edmund during their first and second meetings.

_____

_____

_____

_____

Name _____

Date _____

▲ Analyzing the Literature

Directions: Think about the section you just read. Read each question and state your response with textual evidence.

1. What do the children learn about Aslan and the Witch?

_____

_____

_____

_____

2. Why does Edmund lie to himself on his way to the Witch's castle?

_____

_____

_____

_____

3. Why is the changing of the weather so important in the story?

_____

_____

_____

_____

4. Why does the Witch treat Edmund so differently from their first meeting?

_____

_____

_____

_____

Name _____

Date _____

Reader Response

Directions: Choose one of the following prompts about this section to answer. Be sure you include a topic sentence in your response, use textual evidence to support your opinion, and provide a strong conclusion that summarizes your opinion.

Writing Prompts

- **Narrative Piece**—Peter, Susan, and Lucy receive gifts from Father Christmas that might be useful later in the story. Write about a time you received a gift that was useful. Include when it was given to you and how you used it.
- **Informative/Explanatory Piece**—Reread the prophecy about Aslan in the beginning of chapter 8 and write about what you think it means.

_____

_____

_____

_____

_____

_____

_____

_____

_____

_____

_____

_____

_____

_____

Name _____

Date _____

Close Reading the Literature

Directions: Closely reread the section in chapter 8 when Mr. Beaver shares the second prophecy and the children discover Edmund's betrayal. Begin when Mr. Beaver says, "Because of another prophecy . . . ." Continue reading until he says, ". . . something about their eyes." Read each question and then revisit the text to find evidence that supports your answer.

1. According to the text, what is the second prophecy about the castle at Cair Paravel?

   _____

   _____

   _____

2. Using the section, compare the children's feelings when they notice Edmund's disappearance to their feelings after talking with Mr. Beaver.

   _____

   _____

   _____

   _____

3. Use text support to explain why Mr. Beaver does not want to look for Edmund.

   _____

   _____

   _____

4. What "look" does Mr. Beaver say Edmund has?

   _____

   _____

   _____

Name _____

Date _____

Making Connections—Poetic Prophesies

Directions: The prophecy about Aslan is written as a poem. A *diamante poem* is a seven-line poem about two different topics. When it is written, it looks like a diamond. Follow the guidelines below to write a diamante poem. It can be about the book or topics of your choice. Use the example for inspiration.

_____
topic 1

_____ _____
two adjectives about topic 1

_____ _____ _____
three –ing verbs about topic 1

_____ _____ _____ _____
short phrase about topic 1 and short phrase about topic 2

_____ _____ _____
three –ing verbs about topic 2

_____ _____
two adjectives about topic 2

_____
topic 2

• • • • • • • • • • • • • • • • • • • •

Aslan

good, unsafe

returning, saving, ruling

Narnia's King —— Freezing Narnia

tricking, punishing, ruining

cruel, liar

Witch

Name _____

Date _____

Creating with the Story Elements

Directions: Thinking about the story elements of character, setting, and plot in a novel is very important to understanding what is happening and why. Complete **one** of the following activities based on what you've read so far. Be creative and have fun!

Characters

Mr. Beaver is a helpful character who shares information about Narnia and other characters. Make a list of at least four things he tells the children.

Setting

As Aslan approaches, the weather begins to change. Divide a piece of paper into two equal sections. On the left side, draw Narnia in the winter. On the right side, draw spring's arrival in Narnia as the children and Mr. and Mrs. Beaver walk through the woods.

Plot

Peter, Susan, and Lucy each receive a gift from Father Christmas. Draw each gift they receive. Under the drawings, write a prediction about how or when the gifts will be used.

Vocabulary Overview

Ten key words from this section are provided below with definitions and sentences about how the words are used in the book. Choose one of the vocabulary activity sheets (pages 45 or 46) for students to complete as they read this section. Monitor students as they work to ensure the definitions they have found are accurate and relate to the text. Finally, discuss these important vocabulary words with students. If you think these words or other words in the section warrant more time devoted to them, there are suggestions in the introduction for other vocabulary activities (page 5).

Word	Definition	Sentence about Text
pavilion (ch. 12)	a building with open sides often used as shelter at a park	There is a **pavilion** on one side of the Stone Table.
rampant (ch. 12)	standing on one hind foot with one foreleg raised above the other and the head in profile	The pole has a banner with a red **rampant** lion fluttering in the breeze.
mantle (ch. 13)	a long, sleeveless robe	The Witch takes off her **mantle** and shows her bare, white arms.
forfeit (ch. 13)	to lose or give up something as a punishment because of a rule	Edmund's life is **forfeit** to the Witch.
renounced (ch. 13)	gave up something in a formal way	The Witch has **renounced** her claim on Edmund's blood.
roused (ch. 14)	caused a tired or uninterested person to become active	Aslan is thinking about something else, but he **rouses** himself by shaking his mane.
rabble (ch. 14)	a large group of people who could become violent	The **rabble** is enraged when Aslan does not move.
whet (ch. 14)	to make something sharper or stronger	The Witch begins to **whet** her knife.
pact (ch. 14)	a formal agreement to help people or groups to stop fighting	Aslan and the Witch make a **pact**.
appeased (ch. 14)	made happy by giving something that is wanted	The Witch knows the Deep Magic will be **appeased**.

Name _____

Date _____

Understanding Vocabulary Words

Directions: The following words appear in this section of the book. Use context clues and reference materials to determine an accurate definition for each word.

Word	Definition
pavilion (ch. 12)	
rampant (ch. 12)	
mantle (ch. 13)	
forfeit (ch. 13)	
renounced (ch. 13)	
roused (ch. 14)	
rabble (ch. 14)	
whet (ch. 14)	
pact (ch. 14)	
appeased (ch. 14)	

Name _____

Date _____

During-Reading Vocabulary Activity

Directions: As you read these chapters, record at least eight important words on the lines below. Try to find interesting, difficult, intriguing, special, or funny words. Your words can be long or short. They can be hard or easy to spell. After each word, use context clues in the text and reference materials to define the word.

- _____

- _____

- _____

- _____

- _____

- _____

- _____

- _____

- _____

- _____

- _____

Directions: Respond to these questions about the words in this section.

1. Why must Edmund **forfeit** his life to the Witch?

   _____

   _____

2. How will the Deep Magic be **appeased**?

   _____

   _____

Analyzing the Literature

Provided below are discussion questions you can use in small groups, with the whole class, or for written assignments. Each question is given at two levels so you can choose the right question for each group of students. Activity sheets with these questions are provided (pages 48–49) if you want students to write their responses. For each question, a few key discussion points are provided for your reference.

Story Element	■ Level 1	▲ Level 2	Key Discussion Points
Character	What does Aslan remind Peter to do after he kills the wolf?	Why do you think Aslan reminds Peter to wipe his sword?	Aslan reminds Peter to wipe his sword because it is still covered with the wolf's blood and hair. Student answers will vary but may include the following: so that the blade will not rust; so that he is ready for the next battle; or to show that the battle is over.
Character	Describe Edmund's actions after speaking with Aslan.	Compare Edmund's actions after speaking with Aslan to his actions before their conversation.	After speaking with Aslan, Edmund sincerely apologizes to his siblings for his betrayal. He also continues to look at Aslan regardless of what is going on around him and does not feel the need to speak; he waits to see what Aslan says and does. Before their talk, Edmund feels no respect toward Aslan, is prideful and would not have apologized, and wants to have all the attention.
Plot	What is the pact between the Witch and Aslan?	Why is the Witch willing to take Aslan instead of Edmund?	Aslan agrees that a death is necessary to appease the Deep Magic. He enters into a pact with the Witch and volunteers to take Edmund's place for the punishment. The Witch is willing to have Aslan for the replacement so she can be rid of Aslan and rule Narnia as queen without the threat of his return.
Plot	Why do Susan and Lucy follow Aslan?	How does Aslan show he wants Susan and Lucy to stay with him?	The girls cannot sleep and have bad feelings. They are concerned for Aslan because he seems different and sad. Aslan wants their company and their comfort. He allows them to walk with him and asks them to put their hands on his mane so he can feel them next to him.

Name _____

Date _____

Analyzing the Literature

Directions: Think about the section you just read. Read each question and state your response with textual evidence.

1. What does Aslan remind Peter to do after he kills the wolf?

_____

_____

_____

_____

2. Describe Edmund's actions after speaking with Aslan.

_____

_____

_____

_____

3. What is the pact between the Witch and Aslan?

_____

_____

_____

_____

4. Why do Susan and Lucy follow Aslan?

_____

_____

_____

_____

Name _____

Date _____

▲ Analyzing the Literature

Directions: Think about the section you just read. Read each question and state your response with textual evidence.

1. Why do you think Aslan reminds Peter to wipe his sword?

_____

_____

_____

_____

2. Compare Edmund's actions after speaking with Aslan to his actions before their conversation.

_____

_____

_____

_____

3. Why is the Witch willing to take Aslan instead of Edmund?

_____

_____

_____

_____

4. How does Aslan show he wants Susan and Lucy to stay with him?

_____

_____

_____

_____

Name _____

Date _____

Reader Response

Directions: Choose one of the following prompts about this section to answer. Be sure you include a topic sentence in your response, use textual evidence to support your opinion, and provide a strong conclusion that summarizes your opinion.

Writing Prompts

- **Narrative Piece**—Edmund receives forgiveness from both Aslan and his siblings for his betrayal. Write about a time you received forgiveness from another person or a time when you forgave someone.
- **Opinion/Argument Piece**—Has Aslan made a mistake in sacrificing himself for Edmund? Include examples to support your opinion.

_____

_____

_____

_____

_____

_____

_____

_____

_____

_____

_____

_____

_____

_____

Name _____

Date _____

Close Reading the Literature

Directions: Closely reread the end of chapter 14 when Aslan is being put to death. Begin with, "Lucy and Susan held their breaths waiting for Aslan's roar . . . ." Read until the end of the chapter. Read each question and then revisit the text to find evidence that supports your answer.

1. Give two examples from the text that show Aslan could have saved himself.

   _____

   _____

   _____

   _____

2. According to the section, how is Aslan hurt and humiliated by the rabble?

   _____

   _____

   _____

3. What is Aslan's response to the treatment he receives? Use text evidence in your answer.

   _____

   _____

   _____

4. At the end of this section, what does the Witch threaten to do after Aslan's death?

   _____

   _____

   _____

Name _____

Date _____

Making Connections–Mythical Creatures

Directions: Many mythical creatures and beasts are mentioned in the book. A few examples are fauns, centaurs, unicorns, ogres, and sprites. Choose one of the creatures to research using a book, an online encyclopedia, or another resource. Draw a picture and complete the questions below.

1. Describe the creature.

   _____

   _____

2. What is the culture or history of the creature?

   _____

   _____

3. List two other interesting facts about the creature.

   • _____

   • _____

Name _____

Date _____

Creating with the Story Elements

Directions: Thinking about the story elements of character, setting, and plot in a novel is very important to understanding what is happening and why. Complete **one** of the following activities based on what you've read so far. Be creative and have fun!

Characters

In an earlier section, Aslan is described as being good but not safe. Make a list of at least five other adjectives or phrases that describe him.

Setting

Using the descriptions and details in the text, draw the Stone Table and Pavilion.

Plot

The conversation between Aslan and Edmund is not in the book. Use your imagination and information in the text to write the dialogue of what they might have said to one another.

Vocabulary Overview

Ten key words from this section are provided below with definitions and sentences about how the words are used in the book. Choose one of the vocabulary activity sheets (pages 55 or 56) for students to complete as they read this section. Monitor students as they work to ensure the definitions they have found are accurate and relate to the text. Finally, discuss these important vocabulary words with students. If you think these words or other words in the section warrant more time devoted to them, there are suggestions in the introduction for other vocabulary activities (page 5).

Word	Definition	Sentence about Text
vile (ch. 15)	bad or unpleasant	The **vile** rabble comes sweeping off the hilltop past their hiding place.
fondled (ch. 15)	touched in a gentle way	After Aslan dies, Susan and Lucy kiss and **fondle** his face.
incantation (ch. 15)	words used to make something magical happen	If the Witch looks before the dawn of time, she will read a different **incantation**.
prodigious (ch. 16)	very impressive	The stone lion gives a **prodigious** yawn.
plumage (ch. 16)	feathers covering the body of a bird	The birds that were turned to stone have dazzling **plumage**.
ransacking (ch. 16)	searching for something in a way that causes damage	At last, the **ransacking** of the Witch's fortress ends.
liberated (ch. 16)	freed something from the control of another	The crowd of **liberated** statues runs back to the courtyard.
revelry (ch. 17)	a noisy celebration	That night there is a big feast, **revelry**, and dancing.
brood (ch. 17)	a group of something, often young animals	In the end, the foul **brood** is stamped out.
courtiers (ch. 17)	members of the royal court	They ride until the horses of all the **courtiers** are tired out.

Name _____

Date _____

Understanding Vocabulary Words

Directions: The following words appear in this section of the book. Use context clues and reference materials to determine an accurate definition for each word.

Word	Definition
vile (ch. 15)	
fondled (ch. 15)	
incantation (ch. 15)	
prodigious (ch. 16)	
plumage (ch. 16)	
ransacking (ch. 16)	
liberated (ch. 16)	
revelry (ch. 17)	
brood (ch. 17)	
courtiers (ch. 17)	

Name _____

Date _____

During-Reading Vocabulary Activity

Directions: As you read these chapters, choose five important words from the story. Use these words to complete the word flow chart below. On each arrow, write a word. In each box, explain how the connected pair of words relates to each other. An example for the words *incantation* and *prodigious* has been done for you.

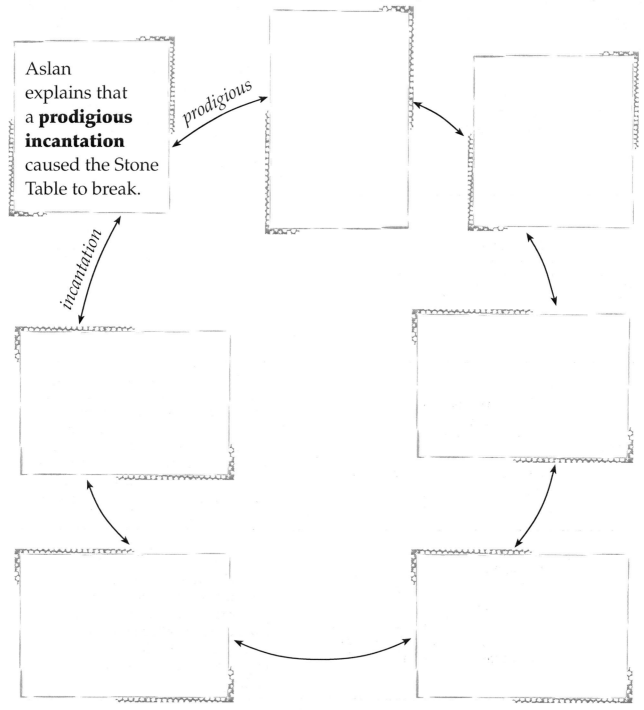

Aslan explains that a **prodigious incantation** caused the Stone Table to break.

Analyzing the Literature

Provided below are discussion questions you can use in small groups, with the whole class, or for written assignments. Each question is given at two levels so you can choose the right question for each group of students. Activity sheets with these questions are provided (pages 58–59) if you want students to write their responses. For each question, a few key discussion points are provided for your reference.

Story Element	■ Level 1	▲ Level 2	Key Discussion Points
Character	What does Aslan do at the Witch's castle?	Why does Aslan go to the Witch's castle?	At the castle, Aslan breathes on the stone statues and breaks the spell so they are alive again. He frees them so they are no longer her captives and can fight in the battle against the Witch.
Setting	How does Edmund stop the Witch from turning everyone into stone?	How does Edmund show he is brave and clever during the battle?	Instead of attacking the Witch, Edmund destroys her wand so she cannot turn anything to stone. This shows he is clever. He shows he is brave by fighting different creatures and the Witch herself, even though he is injured.
Plot	What happens when Peter, Susan, Edmund, and Lucy are chasing the white stag?	How do Peter, Susan, Edmund, and Lucy find their way back to our world?	While chasing the white stag, they find a tree which has grown around a lamp-post. At first they are confused, but then they remember they have seen it before. They walk through the woods, which turn into coats, and stumble out of wardrobe. They are children again, and it is the same hour as when they left.
Plot	When the children confess their adventures to the Professor, what is his reaction?	When the children confess their adventures to the Professor, what advice does he give them?	The Professor believes them and does not find their story strange at all. He advises the children to not purposely try entering Narnia again. They might find their way back when they aren't looking for it. He tells them they will return to Narnia again because, "Once a King, always a King."

Name _____

Date _____

▪ Analyzing the Literature

Directions: Think about the section you just read. Read each question and state your response with textual evidence.

1. What does Aslan do at the Witch's castle?

   _____

   _____

   _____

   _____

2. How does Edmund stop the Witch from turning everyone into stone?

   _____

   _____

   _____

   _____

3. What happens when Peter, Susan, Edmund, and Lucy are chasing the white stag?

   _____

   _____

   _____

   _____

4. When the children confess their adventures to the Professor, what is his reaction?

   _____

   _____

   _____

Name _____

Date _____

▲ Analyzing the Literature

Directions: Think about the section you just read. Read each question and state your response with textual evidence.

1. Why does Aslan go to the Witch's castle?

    _____

    _____

    _____

    _____

2. How does Edmund show he is brave and clever during the battle?

    _____

    _____

    _____

    _____

3. How do Peter, Susan, Edmund, and Lucy find their way back to our world?

    _____

    _____

    _____

    _____

4. When the children confess their adventures to the Professor, what advice does he give them?

    _____

    _____

    _____

    _____

Name _____

Date _____

Reader Response

Directions: Choose one of the following prompts about this section to answer. Be sure you include a topic sentence in your response, use textual evidence to support your opinion, and provide a strong conclusion that summarizes your opinion.

Writing Prompts

- **Opinion/Argument Piece**—Susan does not think Edmund should know about Aslan's sacrifice for him. Do you agree or disagree with her? Include examples to support your opinion.
- **Informative/Explanatory Piece**—Pretend you are one of the adult Kings or Queens. Write a brief memoir of your time as a ruler of Narnia. Use information from the book as you tell about your reign.

_____

_____

_____

_____

_____

_____

_____

_____

_____

_____

_____

_____

_____

Name _____

Date _____

Close Reading the Literature

Directions: Closely reread when Aslan comes back to life in chapter 15. Begin when Lucy says, "They're doing something worse to *Him*!" Read until, ". . . the girls no longer felt in the least tired or hungry or thirsty." Read each question and then revisit the text to find evidence that supports your answer.

1. Before Aslan reappears in this section, what do Susan and Lucy think has happened?

   _____

   _____

   _____

   _____

2. In this section, why do the girls feel as frightened as they are glad?

   _____

   _____

   _____

   _____

3. According to the text, how is Aslan able to come back to life?

   _____

   _____

   _____

4. As Aslan's strength returns, what does he do?

   _____

   _____

   _____

Name _____

Date _____

Making Connections–Character Class Book

Directions: You and your classmates will be creating a class book with details of the characters in the book. Choose a character from the book. In the space below, write a paragraph about your character. On a separate sheet of paper, draw and color a picture of him or her. The paragraph should do the following:

- Introduce the character's name and species.
- Explain the personality of the character.
- Tell about any important things the character does in the book.
- Share any other interesting information.

Character I Chose: _____

_____

_____

_____

_____

_____

_____

_____

_____

_____

_____

_____

_____

_____

Name _____

Date _____

Creating with the Story Elements

Directions: Thinking about the story elements of character, setting, and plot in a novel is very important to understanding what is happening and why. Complete **one** of the following activities based on what you've read so far. Be creative and have fun!

Characters

Edmund changes a great deal from the beginning to the end of the book. Create a Venn diagram to compare and contrast his character. Label the left side "beginning of book" and the right side "end of book." Put at least five words or phrases on each side and at least three words or phrases in the middle section.

Setting

Draw the scene when Aslan, Susan, and Lucy go to the Witch's castle and free all of the creatures frozen in stone. Use details from the book and your imagination.

Plot

As adult Kings and Queens, the children speak very differently. Create a comic strip that illustrates the scene when they find the lamp-post. Have them speak regularly instead of like Kings and Queens.

Name _____

Date _____

Post-Reading Theme Thoughts

Directions: Read each of the statements in the first column. Choose a main character from *The Lion, the Witch and the Wardrobe*. Think about that character's point of view. From that character's perspective, decide if the character would agree or disagree with the statements. Record the character's opinion by marking an *X* in Agree or Disagree for each statement. Explain your choices in the fourth column using textual evidence.

Character I Chose: _____

Statement	Agree	Disagree	Explain Your Answer
You should not believe something unless you see it for yourself.			
People who have done bad things should be forgiven.			
Sacrifice is a way to show love.			
Children are too young to do brave and noble things.			

Name _____

Date _____

Culminating Activity: Narnia–Read All About It!

Overview: *The Lion, the Witch and the Wardrobe* is a fantasy book with a lot of action. There are good and evil characters, great battles, and daring rescues. A newspaper would be a fun way to communicate to all creatures in Narnia the exciting events that have happened.

Directions: Read through the different parts of a newspaper. The front page and letter to the editor are required pages to include. Choose either entertainment or lifestyle from option 1; choose either classifieds or comics from option 2. Make your choices below by circling the parts you wish to include in your newspaper. Be thinking of ideas from the book to include for each page.

Required: Front Page	Required: Letter to the Editor
• contains facts • written about an important event that has happened recently	• contains opinions about a topic • letter to editor written by reader and sent to newspaper
Option 1: Entertainment	**Option 1: Lifestyle**
• contains information about entertaining things happening in the area • examples include concerts, plays, games, movies, and sports events	• contains information about people's lives and homes • examples include cooking, decorating, fashion, travel, and advice
Option 2: Classifieds	**Option 2: Comics**
• a list of short advertisements • examples include available jobs, cars, apartments, and houses for sale or rent	• a series of funny illustrations that tell a short story • often use dialogue balloons and thought bubbles

Name _____

Date _____

Culminating Activity:
Narnia–Read All About It! *(cont.)*

Directions: Fill in your choices for the sections in the newspaper (the first two sections have been done for you). In the boxes provided, write ideas you have for the information for each section. Use events from the book, but also use your imagination as you create the different sections of your Narnia newspaper.

Front Page	Letter to the Editor
Option 1: _____	**Option 2:** _____

Directions: Every newspaper needs a title, or a *masthead*, on the front page. Usually the name is designed to catch the readers' eyes. From the options below, chose a font for your Narnia newspaper. On another sheet of paper, use your favorite font below to write your own newspaper's name. The sides and tips of markers work well to color and shade in the letters.

Narnia Newspaper

Narnia Newspaper

NARNIA NEWSPAPER

Name _____

Date _____

Comprehension Assessment

Directions: Circle the correct response to each question.

1. What is the meaning of *prophecy* as used in the book?

    A. Deep Magic from the Stone Table

    B. a prediction about things that will happen in Narnia

    C. the return of spring after a long winter

    D. the crowning of Edmund as Prince by the Witch

2. Which detail from the book best supports your answer to question 1?

    E. "At the same time, he noticed that he was feeling much less cold."

    F. ". . . there is a magic deeper still which she did not know."

    G. "I want a nice boy whom I could bring up as a Prince."

    H. "Wrong will be right, when Aslan comes into sight."

3. Write the main idea of the text below in the graphic organizer.

    The Professor: "Either your sister is telling lies, or she is mad, or she is telling the truth. You know she doesn't tell lies and it is obvious that she is not mad."

Main Idea (question 3)

Details (question 4)

Details (question 4)

Comprehension Assessment (cont.)

4. Choose **two** supporting details from those below to add to the graphic organizer on the previous page.

    A. Lucy is more honest than Edmund.

    B. Edmund says Narnia is not real.

    C. The Professor wants the children to use logic.

    D. Just speaking with Lucy proves she is not mad.

5. Which statement best expresses one of the themes of the book?

    E. Forgiving others is important.

    F. Battles are not for children.

    G. People should be prepared for anything.

    H. Useful gifts are the most appropriate.

6. What detail from the book provides the best evidence for your answer to number 5?

    A. "You didn't think we'd set out on a journey with nothing to eat, did you?"

    B. "These are your presents, and they are tools not toys."

    C. "Here is your brother and—there is no need to talk to him about what is past."

    D. "Peter did not feel very brave . . . but that made no difference to what he had to do."

7. What is the purpose of these sentences about Aslan: "Who said anything about safe? 'Course he isn't safe. But he's good. He's the King, I tell you."

    _____

    _____

8. Which other quotation from the story serves a similar purpose?

    E. "People sometimes think a thing cannot be good and terrible at the same time."

    F. "'You have forgotten to clean your sword,' said Aslan."

    G. "At this point Aslan clapped his paws together and called for silence."

    H. "Did you hear what he said? *Us lions*. That means him and me."

Name _____

Date _____

Response to Literature: Heroes of Here and There

Overview: Aslan in *The Lion, the Witch and the Wardrobe* is a character who shows goodness and moral strength. He fights for justice, defends the weak, and dies doing what he feels is right. Many people throughout history have done these same things. Read through a few real-life examples of people who helped make the world a better place.

- *Joan of Arc* (1412–1431)—The French and English fought a very long war. When Joan was 12, she started hearing voices and said it was God. The voice told her she was going to lead the French to victory. At a young age, she became a great military leader.

- *Abraham Lincoln* (1809–1865)—Lincoln was the president of the United States during the Civil War. He freed the slaves and was a strong leader while the North and South battled each other.

- *Mahatma Gandhi* (1869–1948)—England ruled India when Gandhi was young, but India wanted to be a free country. Gandhi encouraged people to fight England's government but to do it peacefully.

- *Martin Luther King Jr.* (1929–1968)—In the 1950s and 1960s in America, people tried to change laws so things would be fair for African Americans. King was a leader of this movement. He did not use violence and believed in love, not hate.

Directions: Select one of these people and compare and contrast him or her to Aslan. In what ways did they try to help others? How did they help change the world? Write a researched essay showing your understanding of the historical figure and how he or she compares to Aslan. Use facts and details about the person, and also cite the novel to support your thinking.

Your essay response to literature should follow these guidelines:
- Be at least 750 words in length.
- Cite information about the historical figure.
- Compare/contrast the person to Aslan.
- Cite at least three references from the novel.
- Provide a conclusion that summarizes your thoughts and findings.

Final essays are due on _____.

Name _____

Date _____

Response to Literature Rubric

Directions: Use this rubric to evaluate student responses.

	Exceptional Writing	Quality Writing	Developing Writing
Focus and Organization	☐ States a clear opinion and elaborates well. Engages the reader from the opening hook through the middle to the conclusion. Demonstrates clear understanding of the intended audience and purpose of the piece.	☐ Provides a clear and consistent opinion. Maintains a clear perspective and supports it through elaborating details. Makes the opinion clear in the opening hook and summarizes well in the conclusion.	☐ Provides an inconsistent point of view. Does not support the topic adequately or misses pertinent information. Provides lack of clarity in the beginning, middle, and conclusion.
Text Evidence	☐ Provides comprehensive and accurate support. Includes relevant and worthwhile text references.	☐ Provides limited support. Provides few supporting text references.	☐ Provides very limited support for the text. Provides no supporting text references.
Written Expression	☐ Uses descriptive and precise language with clarity and intention. Maintains a consistent voice and uses an appropriate tone that supports meaning. Uses multiple sentence types and transitions well between ideas.	☐ Uses a broad vocabulary. Maintains a consistent voice and supports a tone and feelings through language. Varies sentence length and word choices.	☐ Uses a limited and unvaried vocabulary. Provides an inconsistent or weak voice and tone. Provides little to no variation in sentence type and length.
Language Conventions	☐ Capitalizes, punctuates, and spells accurately. Demonstrates complete thoughts within sentences, with accurate subject-verb agreement. Uses paragraphs appropriately and with clear purpose.	☐ Capitalizes, punctuates, and spells accurately. Demonstrates complete thoughts within sentences and appropriate grammar. Paragraphs are properly divided and supported.	☐ Incorrectly capitalizes, punctuates, and spells. Uses fragmented or run-on sentences. Utilizes poor grammar overall. Paragraphs are poorly divided and developed.

The responses provided here are just examples of what the students may answer. Many accurate responses are possible for the questions throughout this unit.

During-Reading Vocabulary Activity— Section 1: Chapters 1–4 (page 16)

1. Mr. Tumnus has a **melancholy** voice because he is upset that he has tricked Lucy.

2. Peter thinks Lucy's story is a **hoax** because it does not seem possible that she visited Narnia.

Close Reading the Literature—Section 1: Chapters 1–4 (page 21)

1. Edmund wants more Turkish Delight because it is enchanted. Whoever eats it will want to eat it forever.

2. Edmund is selfish because he does not want his brother or sisters to be made a duke and duchesses.

3. Edmund will find the Witch's castle by walking in between the two hills in the distance.

4. The Witch's excuse is that the Fauns have spread nasty, untrue stories about her.

Making Connections—Section 1: Chapters 1–4 (page 22)

1. Anderson shelters are outdoors under gardens and have wavy steel walls. Morrison shelters are indoor steel tables with cage-like sides.

2. The children were evacuated from big cities because that is where the bombing was happening.

3. Problems the children faced were missing their families or being scared of living with strangers.

During-Reading Vocabulary Activity— Section 2: Chapters 5–7 (page 26)

1. The Professor wonders if **logic** is taught because he feels as though Peter and Susan are not using any.

2. They talk under the **boughs** because Mr. Beaver does not want others to hear them, including the trees.

Close Reading the Literature—Section 2: Chapters 5–7 (page 31)

1. The very serious thing is to accuse an honest person of lying.

2. The Professor's logical explanation is that Lucy is either lying, crazy, or telling the truth.

3. The detail is that Lucy says she was gone for hours, but it really was only moments. The Professor feels if she had been lying, she would have hidden for a while before telling the story.

4. The Professor's plan is for everyone to mind their own business.

Making Connections—Section 2: Chapters 5–7 (page 32)

1. most permeable—gravel; least permeable—clay

2. To be less permeable, the pieces of the material must be very small and very close together.

3. Answers may vary, but an example is: If all three were used, the dam would be even less permeable, and it would take longer for the water to seep through.

Close Reading the Literature—Section 3: Chapters 8–11 (page 41)

1. The second prophecy states there are four thrones for two Daughters of Eve and two Sons of Adam. When they rule, it will be the end of the Witch's life.

2. At first, the children are very concerned about Edmund and want to organize a search party. After Mr. Beaver says Edmund has betrayed them, they are stunned but know he is right.

3. Mr. Beaver does not want to look for Edmund because he knows immediately that Edmund has betrayed them, joined the Witch's side, and has gone to her castle.

4. Mr. Beaver says Edmund has the look of someone who has met the Witch and has tasted her food.

During-Reading Vocabulary Activity—Section 4: Chapters 12–14 (page 46)

1. Edmund must forfeit his life to the Witch because he is a traitor.

2. The Deep Magic will be appeased when the traitor dies.

Close Reading the Literature—Section 4: Chapters 12–14 (page 51)

1. Aslan could have saved himself when the rabble tied him up or when they muzzled him.

2. Aslan's mane is cut off, he is tied up, and the rabble hit, kick, spit, and jeer at him.

3. Aslan's reaction is to be quiet and still. He does not fight back or resist in any way, letting them do whatever they want to him.

4. The Witch threatens to kill Edmund anyway after Aslan dies because she will be Queen and nothing will stop her. She says Aslan's death will have changed nothing.

Close Reading the Literature—Section 5: Chapters 15–17 (page 61)

1. Susan and Lucy fear more magic has been done and Aslan's body has been taken.

2. The girls feel frightened because although they see Aslan, they are worried that he is a ghost.

3. Aslan comes back to life because of the deeper magic that says when a blameless person takes the place of a traitor, the Stone Table will crack and death will work backwards.

4. Aslan plays with the girls. They chase him and they romp and roll around together.

Comprehension Assessment (pages 67–68)

1. B. a prediction about things that will happen in Narnia

2. H. "Wrong will be right, when Aslan comes into sight."

3. Main Idea: Lucy is telling the truth about Narnia.

4. A. Lucy is more honest than Edmund; D. Just speaking with Lucy proves she is not mad.

5. E. Forgiving others is important.

6. C. "Here is your brother and—there is no need to talk to him about what is past."

7. The sentences let the reader know that although Aslan is wild and might scare the children, he is good and will always do the right thing to help others.

8. E. "People sometimes think a thing cannot be good and terrible at the same time."